FOOD-RELATED STORIES

GABY MELIAN

PENGUIN WORKSHOP

To my mom, you were right:

el tiempo es un verdadero bromista—GM

PENGUIN WORKSHOP
An imprint of Penguin Random House LLC, New York

First published in the United States of America by Penguin Workshop,
an imprint of Penguin Random House LLC, New York, 2021

Text copyright © 2021 by Maria Gabriela Melian
Illustrations copyright © 2021 by Penguin Random House LLC

Visit us online at penguinrandomhouse.com.

Library of Congress Control Number: 2021018230

Manufactured in China

ISBN 9780593223499   10 9 8 7 6 5 4 3 2 1 HH

PROLOGUE

My younger brother, Gonzalo, and I had not seen each other for at least seven years. For reasons that are hard to explain, I stopped traveling to Argentina in 2009 and hadn't seen him much since. As he stepped off the plane to a cold, bitter winter in New Jersey, I wished our reunion was under different circumstances. It was 2016, a few days before Martin Luther King Jr. weekend and the biggest nor'easter we'd seen in decades. And we had to do the unthinkable: We were saying goodbye to our mother.

The last day our mother was conscious was on that Saturday. She spoke softly with my brother and me, chit-chatting here and there with what little voice she had left—as you do when you're trying to avoid the monstrous, glaring elephant in the room. At one point, Gonzalo stared out the window and asked if it was *really* going to snow. He really wanted to see snow. "Don't worry, you are going to see tons of it," Mom whispered, faintly smiling.

She died that Monday, January 18, as the snow quietly started to lie on the ground and lasted for what felt like ages. One of the many times my mom kept her word no matter what.

Everything afterward felt rushed. Goodbyes usually feel that way. They come too soon and rarely do you want to say them. The day after she died, we decided to go to her apartment. She lived in a senior citizen building in Jersey City, and we managed to get to her place, even though the snow made it almost impossible to walk the six blocks that separated my apartment from hers.

So there we were, alone in her studio that she had proudly decorated and filled up to the brim with plants and pillows and her huge collection of owls. The apartment was small and had that very unique scent of a senior citizen's home. You know the one.

Even my mother knew the one. She often joked that it smelled "viejo." Then again, her studio also had the faint scent of incense and cigarettes, the latter of which is what killed her in the end.

It was hard to be confronted with her memories and the dust that began to form around them. Having to pack up her place proved even harder. While my brother was trying to comprehend how our mom spent her last months, and how she lived in such a tiny place, I was trying to figure out how in the world I was going to empty it. He wanted to save everything and wait. I wanted all of this to be done yesterday. I was too close to it.

We started going through her things without a clear idea how we were going to do it. We weren't even sure where to properly start. So I went for what I knew best: I started with the fridge. After all, her fridge was my domain, and I had been organizing it for months. I knew my mission as I stepped into the kitchen.

Up until the day she was hospitalized for the last time, I went to her place daily with food. I made sure to fill up her fridge with things that brought her joy during the course of her cancer treatment. I knew what she liked to eat and what she did not. I bought everything from strawberry ice cream to vanilla yogurt to watermelon. In fact, I used to make tiny melon balls and fill up two- or three-quart containers so she always had something fresquito to eat.

It was the first time in a little bit that I had checked her freezer. It held many things: pints of ice cream toppling over each other, Ziploc bags with bread for her morning toast, coffee, ice cube trays, and, of course, the one leftover meal—her fish.

My mom only ever cooked for a crowd, which seems to be genetic because I've had the same issue for years. I recently learned to scale down my recipes for one or two people, but she never did. She would make large batches of food and freeze them until she remembered she had them, or until I showed up hungry. And there it was: my mom's fish, her special recipe that she made for us. Oven-baked white fillet of fish (usually cod or whiting), over thinly sliced potatoes, red peppers, onions, and spices that vary from time to time depending on the day—from dry oregano to thyme—and, of course, olive oil, salt, and pepper. It was her caballito de batalla. Her war horse. The dish we always liked and never complained about. A winner every time.

Tears began to stream down my face as I stared at the frozen Pyrex container wrapped in plastic. I wanted to somehow hold on to this (to hold on to her) for just a little while longer. But we also had loads of packing up to do and I was starving. So we went for it. My brother and I stopped what we were doing and sat down to eat together. And for a brief moment, it was as if my mom was with us, keeping her word and taking care of us one last time.

Since then, I've made her fish numerous times. I can easily replicate the recipe and only now do I realize what a gift that is—to have had my mom pass down something so personal and so precious to me.

I believe food makes things better, no matter how frozen or simple it is. The act of eating, in the company of others or alone, is a caring act. Caring for others but also caring for yourself. After all, food is what we all have in common. We all need to eat! But as we all well know, it is so much more than that. Food has rescued me in many moments—and not only because I sold food to survive. I cook to entertain; I cook to be liked; I cook to be loved.

I've made my mom's fish countless times, but it's never tasted as good as on that cold January day. That was just one of the many ways food has saved my life.

FOOD-RELATED STORIES

FOOD IS A STORY.

Every story has a smell. I recently learned that there is a name for people like me. Or rather, for what I do. What I do is smell everything. Yes, *everything*: near, far, here, there. I can smell it all. Some call it hypersensitivity. I call it my lucky charm.

My nose has become an archive for my childhood memories. Whenever I talk to my brother or my three cousins and we reminiscence about our childhood, I am the one who remembers the smell of the story above all else.

We all grew up together in a tight-knit circle in Buenos Aires, Argentina. Buenos Aires has a very distinctive scent that stays with you forever. It smells like mildew, coffee, and cigarettes. But some days, depending on the season, Buenos Aires smells like jasmine, my favorite flower. If you were a young porteño like me (that's what Buenos Aires natives are called because it's a port city), those were the best days—the early October days right around my birthday.

The five of us did everything together. We lived in the same neighborhood and went to the same school. Most days after school, we spent the afternoons with my Abuela Porota. My Abuela Porota's house was tiny: a small two-bedroom apartment with a patio on Calle Cochabamba in San Telmo. San Telmo is one of the oldest neighborhoods of Buenos Aires, lined with cobblestone streets that are full of cafés, street murals, and antique stores. And even though Abuela Porota's house was tiny, somehow she managed to raise three daughters there and, years later, had the five of us together every afternoon wreaking havoc. We would do homework, watch cartoons, and, of course, make a mess. Well, she called it a mess. We called it "cooking." Every story has two sides.

Abuela Porota's house always smelled clean (read: like bleach and floor wax), and I've loved that smell ever since. As you entered the living room, there was a small twin bed in the sitting area that doubled as my youngest tia's bed for many years. To your left, there was a small corridor with the master bedroom on one side and the kitchen right across. My abuela was always brewing or boiling something, even if it was just water for tea. Off the kitchen, there was a second, smaller patio, referred to as a lavadero, because it had a big outdoor sink and a clothesline. She also had a pantry on the patio. The pantry couldn't have been bigger than a cabinet, but I remember it being huge. Probably because what was inside made a world of difference to a future chef-in-training: That was where she kept the flour, sugar, eggs, and spices. My cousins, my brother, and I would experiment, talk, and laugh while a big cloud of flour formed over our heads. Abuela was cool enough to let us do it, but smart enough to make us do it outside.

I still remember the smell of wet flour—the smell of musty, bubbling, raw yeast. An experiment waiting to be shaped and cared for by my abuela's warm hands. She would stand at a very small table (that could fold into an even smaller table) and knead at the wet flour. As a child, I was always curious about what she was making, what her creations would look like. On one of those occasions, she was making her famous handmade ravioli.

I have to stop here. I am sure most people have eaten ravioli in their life: good, bad, mediocre, or even out of a can. You know, the kind where the filling is an unrecognizable cheesy-flavored mush. But I wish that all of you, at least once in your life, would've gotten the chance to experience my abuela's ravioli.

Her dough had the perfect balance: elastic but also strong enough to hold the filling neatly packed inside. Her fillings varied because the way we cooked would change as we approached the end of the month, and the meals started to be heavy on potatoes, rice, dry pasta, and, of course, polenta. But her most decadent and famous ravioli among our family was her ravioles de seso.

Seso is the brain. Cow brain to be exact. I recently called my cousin Pablo and my brother to ask them about the food-related memories we all shared

18

(because, like me, they love to cook and are often my source of inspiration), and they, too, remembered the brain ravioli. They also admitted that, unfortunately, no one makes them anymore. "Pity," I replied. Perhaps it is a lack of time or space. Or maybe they have suspicions about the quality of the cow brain, since these days, conversations with your local butcher are few and far between. I am sure that at the time that my abuela was making them, she knew exactly where the brains had been, and how to clean and cook them without having to look at a recipe or watch a video, simply because she did not have such a thing.

But her ravioli was a little square cloud of magic, and she'd often let us help her make them. She'd usually prepare the dish on Sundays because a pasta dish is a traditional Sunday lunch in Argentina. (Some may disagree with me and say that it is actually the asado, our barbecue, that is our traditional Sunday lunch dish. But for that, you need an outdoor space and nice weather. So I stick by my trusted pasta and ravioli.) Nothing is closer to a labor of love than making pasta. It's even more special if the pasta is filled.

To make ravioli, you need a bit of table space and a steady hand. After you roll out the dough, you carefully portion the filling in a straight line to keep the same distance between each little bit of filling. In my abuela's case, the filling was ground cow brain cooked in butter and olive oil, and liberally seasoned with salt and pepper. Then, of course, comes the hard part: placing the top layer onto the filling, which seals the dreamy ravioli. The secret is to carefully lay it down with one hand while you softly press with the other, not allowing any air bubbles to remain inside. It's painstaking but so, so gratifying. I would watch my abuela do this with the same calmness she did everything else around the kitchen. She'd proceed to cut the ravioli with a tiny fluted wheel cutter, and that was when she'd let me help. I needed to be precise. There was no going back and forth with the wheel. There was only one chance, a quick straight cut and on to the next. We'd work together like a well-oiled machine, my grandmother portioning the fillings as I watched along and meticulously cut the dough.

Years later, when I tried to make ravioli for the first

time as a grown-up in culinary school, I knew exactly what I was doing. As I was making them, portioning the filling and cutting the dough, all of the memories of learning how to cook with my abuela rushed back to me. I began to realize that there's a sanctity to the act of sharing a recipe. It's an act that can oftentimes be taken for granted, but it's one that so sneakily becomes the fabric of our lives. Over the years, I would call my Abuela Porota every Sunday to chat with her and my Tia Susy, who was my mom's oldest sister and one of the best cooks I've ever known. We would always compare notes, and I tried to get her to narrate recipes for me, recipes she had memorized and never measured. "You know, just put the one cup of this and half a cup of that," she would say. But I knew that the cup she was referring to was not a measuring cup, but rather her green, black, and orange teacup that survived from her wedding china set and was always sitting on the cupboard like a trophy.

Passed down from one person to the next, from one generation to the next, these recipes are our stories. They are the way we keep ourselves afloat, a way to process and organize the thousands of memories that hold us. It's another way for us to remember and cherish moments of comfort and joy.

Because let's be real: My nose is pretty good. But it can only do so much.

FOOD IS AN ADVENTURE.

The day I arrived in New York City was very cold. It was December 13, 1996. My boyfriend at the time, Lester, and I landed early in the morning, and it was my second time in John F. Kennedy Airport, a place that brought about so many emotions for me, from fear to joy. I'm of the belief that the importance of an airport cannot be measured by how many flights it has or how clean it is. It should be measured by the emotion that it brings for people, and for me, JFK was the happiest place on earth. I was excited to visit my family and even more excited to see my mom, who had moved to New York City six months earlier. I couldn't wait to hug her after such a long time.

The plan was for Lester and me to stay a few months,

practice our English, then go back to Argentina, where we both had jobs waiting for us, a nice apartment, a dog that we had left behind with my dad, friends, and a lot of plants. Well, that was the plan, anyway.

I was also a recent college graduate. I went to the oldest journalism school in Buenos Aires, Instituto Grafotécnico. I was fascinated with journalism from a young age—ever since I was twelve years old and the ten-week undeclared war between Argentina and the United Kingdom over the Falkland Islands (Islas Malvinas) had us completely glued to our TV sets. Back then, we would watch the news from three or four various channels that were pretty much controlled by Argentina's military government. In fact, we regularly listened to the radio station from our bordering country, Uruguay, to find out a bit more of what was going on. From then on, I wanted to be able to help somehow by telling the truth. I wanted to be on the ground, investigating, and learning about the issues at hand. But as I graduated college with a journalism degree, I realized that that path was not necessarily the most popular career choice in Argentina. I wanted to explore where that path could take me in New York City, a place I had dreamed about for as long as I could remember.

That wasn't the first time I had set foot in New York City. I had traveled there with my mom a few years before to visit my mom's sister, her kids, and her husband. We stayed for almost a month and ended up spending Christmas there. I have to admit that it was my first time celebrating Christmas with real snow. I had seen snow in the south of Argentina, but never in December because summer is usually in full swing at that time. In fact, my family once decorated our Christmas tree in Buenos Aires with fake snow, a tradition that ended as quickly as it started because of the mess it made.

I immediately fell in love with the city: the people, the colorful skyline, the gray asphalt streets, the squirrels. I fell in love with every iconic thing the city had to offer, from Rockefeller Center and its ice-skating rink to Central Park to the Empire State Building and the Chrysler Building with its eagle gargoyles. It felt surreal, especially when you'd grown up watching movies set in New York City. I was hooked for life. I immediately wanted to find out if the city had a smell, too.

On one of those eternally tiresome tourist walks with my mom, I realized that New York City did, indeed, have a particular smell. And no, it's not the smell of pee in the subway on a hot summer day. For me, the smell of the city is the smell of steaming hot salty pretzels from the Central Park street vendors. The first time I ever had a pretzel in my life was by the Metropolitan Museum of Art. I was presented with this knot-shaped bread covered in salt flakes so big they looked like glass shards. I had never seen anything like it before. Then, like magic, the vendor proceeded to offer me mustard, a staple food in my refrigerator to this day (only ever to be outmatched by butter). I thought someone was kidding me when I was given a piece of salty warm bread with mustard. How completely genius!

I wanted to keep searching for more smells and ways to connect myself to this city. As I munched on my pretzel and looked up at the imposing structure of the Met before us, my senses were eager to explore, determined to experience everything possible. I wanted to see the Met in its entirety, which if you've ever been to that museum and walked up those enormous entrance stairs, you know is certainly impossible. Knowing this and having received detailed advice from friends and family, I was still determined. I decided to tackle the Met like I would a recipe: Read the ingredients of the building and meticulously look at the map of each floor. Decide what to "prep and cook" first, when to stop, and, of course, when to take a break to eat (and go to the bathroom). Then, proceed onward. This adventure took me to the museum seven days in a row, skipping one day that the museum was closed. By the time I was done, I could've easily taken someone from the Temple of Dendur to the Christmas tree without blinking or getting lost once.

When I turned twenty-five and finished my journalism degree in Buenos Aires, I was almost certain that I wanted to come back and stay in New York City for at least six months. My dream was to come here, find a job, probably at a Spanish newspaper (because, you know, my English was a little bit dull), and then take it from there. *Practice my English, get a job, really explore New York City, and then go back to Argentina*, I kept telling myself, almost like a mantra. Again, that was the plan, anyway.

The first few weeks, Lester and I were so in love with the city. We moved into my aunt's place in SoHo, but as the holidays came and went, it was time for us to move out and find a place of our own. I started looking for jobs, and that was when reality hit. I found a job as a nanny, and we ended up finding an apartment in Jackson Heights, Queens, off the 7 Train.

We lasted in that apartment maybe two months. We didn't have much, just a mattress on the floor in a spare room in someone's house. There were nights when I couldn't do anything but cry and think about what we left behind—and how far away our dreams started to seem.

The only thing that truly brought me peace was my walk from the train station to my apartment. Anyone who has immigrated to New York at some point gets a tour of Jackson Heights. The reason for this is because you can find a little piece of home everywhere you turn. I felt like I was discovering something new every day. As I walked home, I would listen to the music blasting from the various street corners, stores, and restaurants—the melodies bouncing and somersaulting over one another. I listened to folks speaking in Spanish, overheard infectious laughter and women gossiping at the laundromat. So you can only imagine how happy I was when I discovered that right next to the subway station, right there on 90th Street and Roosevelt Avenue, was an Argentine bakery, Buenos Aires Bakery, known to locals as "La Buenos Aires."

I immediately felt welcome. Everything was familiar, the voices, the colors, the smells. I was so happy that by my fifth visit, I found myself drinking a mate cocido and talking to the manager, Haydeé. She was an older woman with a strong Argentine accent and a witty sense of humor, who wore a signature red lipstick. She had lived in Queens for thirty-five years and was well-known in the community. We became good friends, and one day, she offered me a job to work at the counter of the bakery. I was hesitant at first because the pay wasn't much. But the feeling of home, and all the pastries I wanted, sealed the deal. I worked there for a few months, but I had time to observe and learn a little bit at the bakery. I learned tricks on how to make facturas, a traditional Argentinian pastry, from the head baker, who let me watch the back of the house. I learned how a business was run. But above all, I learned how a business becomes the fabric of a community. How food can ground us even in our shakier moments. In fact, I stayed at that job even after we moved back to Manhattan. I made life-long friends in that bakery, and finally, after months of what seemed like an adventure to nowhere, I felt at home.

FOOD IS PATIENCE.

It's a product of a slow and steady mixture of the elements—of water, of air, of earth, and of fire. Cooking is a process that cannot be rushed, even if sometimes you'd like for things to go just a little bit faster.

I am known for having an impatient personality at times. But not in a bad sense. More like in the way that a tornado crosses in front of you, slightly stops for a second to compliment your shoes, and continues its way to the next stop. Always moving, always doing something or the other, always looking forward.

When you are young, nothing seems to stop you, or at least, that is how I see it now. Nothing seemed to stop me. Or maybe it's that I did not want to stop.

Coming to New York City felt like an easy decision,

and deciding to stay was an easy decision, too. Staying meant that I could keep learning about all that New York City had to offer, discover more about myself, and, of course, try all of the fruits, veggies, chocolates, and nuts in the world. The best part was that I didn't have to go far. Everything was right here, within arm's reach in front of me.

When I arrived in New York City, my mom wanted to show me everything. She had only been living in the city for six months, but she knew Chinatown, SoHo, and the West Village better than even some locals. Her excitement to show me everything about the city was infectious, and one of the things she insisted on showing me was the food. *All* of the food. Every delectable confection on every street in every corner of this city. And my first taste of all the city's wonders happened when she introduced me to none other than the Gourmet Garage.

The Gourmet Garage is now a minichain of supermarkets all over the city, but in the 1990s, it was a small neighborhood place in SoHo that had a hidden treasure beyond my wildest dreams. I couldn't believe my eyes when I saw the amount of different olives and cheeses and specialty cookies *and* candy *and* ingredients that I couldn't pronounce. On top of it all, you were allowed to try anything you wanted. My head exploded, so much so that I applied to work there twice, but they never called me back. Nevertheless, I wanted to taste it all.

Gourmet Garage was the start, and after that, I visited every single specialty food store in the area. My outings were always around a food destination and not even necessarily a restaurant because I couldn't afford it. My favorite places to go were New York City's indoor and outdoor markets where the deliciousness was endless and the vendors would let you try anything. I knew I wanted to cook and eat all of these new flavors. Above all, I wanted to put a name to my passion. I wanted to become a chef.

Culinary school was never in my plan. (You remember that silly little thing called "the plan"?) Never in a million years would I have thought that I would become a chef, and never, ever a chef trained in New York City. Recipes never felt technical to me.

They were always created through word of mouth, a symphony of flavors that started with a conversation, a thought, an idea. I still think about recipes in this way. When I teach cooking to people, especially to young students, I often talk to them about the need for having a flavor profile. It's a term that I learned when I was studying but something that I used all my life without knowing its name. A flavor profile is like a tiny filing cabinet right between your nose, your eyes, and your tongue that functions on demand whenever you experience taste. It sounds silly, but if I said the word "chocolate," chances are, you know the flavor and your preference toward it . . . unless you have a serious allergy to it. Then please stay away. Oftentimes when I think of food, I use this filing cabinet of flavor memories. Going to culinary school was a chance to expand that filing cabinet. Where else was I going to have rows and rows of ingredients right within arm's reach? The school was full of chefs with wonderful careers, and there I was ready to absorb it all.

I applied to the Institute of Culinary Education in 2003 because of an ad in the *Village Voice*. Back then, they offered a work-study program, which meant that I would have to study and also complete thirteen hundred work hours for the school through various jobs, mainly as a steward or stagiaire in the purchasing department. Work-study was not easy. It required long hours of physical work, of washing dishes, and of putting ingredients together for professional and recreational classes. But the reward was being able to observe the professionals, closely watching countless master classes, and having access to ingredients and books. Plus, I met so many people that are my best friends to this day, and that is better than gold.

After completing those hours, stagiaires were granted one tuition-free program in the culinary arts, pastry and baking, or culinary management. I ended up taking all three because I wanted to learn absolutely everything. I also started working, this time around as a chef instructor assistant, and working alongside the teacher and helping the students really sealed the deal for me because it helped me realize that my passion for teaching others to cook was real.

My time in culinary school was a master class

in both physical and mental endurance—a slow, sometimes annoying practice of observation and repetition. I learned so much by watching the instructors and my teachers that today, whenever I teach, I find myself repeating the same ideas that were once shared with me.

By the time I started culinary school, I had also been living in Jersey City for almost five years. I had an apartment on Wayne Street, right in the center of the Historic Downtown. While it took a minute to figure out where in the tristate area felt like home, I can safely say that that Wayne Street apartment was the beginning of a huge, much-needed exhale, a release that I had longed for ever since I arrived in JFK. The reason for this was very simple: It was in that apartment that so many of my food-related stories began. It was where I fed so many of my friends, where we had dinner parties and laughed till our stomachs were full and happy. My want to care for others evolved into this cooking marathon that never ended—nor did I want it to.

My apartment was a one-bedroom, but it had

a great layout, so at any given time I had someone staying over on the couch. Every weekend, I had friends over to eat, especially on Sundays. Argentines are big on getting together with their families on Sundays, and on one particular Sunday, I had set out to make two pots of one of my favorite dishes: guiso de lentejas, otherwise known as lentil stew. But not just any lentil stew. *Our* lentil stew. The way we make it in Argentina, with russet potatoes, onions, parsley, garlic, carrots, sweet potatoes, sausage, pancetta, and spices.

The process of making Argentine lentil stew is simple yet methodical. First, the lentils are soaked for a few hours and thoroughly rinsed. Then the real fun begins: You start by searing the pancetta and the sausages until they get a nice color and render some fat. After you remove those, you add the sofrito—in this case, onions, carrots, parsley, and garlic that have been chopped and diced into very tiny pieces and tossed with oil, salt, pepper, and dry herbs. Then you add some tomato paste and let it cook for a few minutes. By that point the aroma should be so intense that you have to strike while the iron is hot: You quickly add the lentils, some water or broth, tomato sauce, the sausage, pancetta, and veggies, and let it simmer until it's ready.

But back to the story. That Sunday, I set out to make two pots of guiso de lentejas: one with all the meat fixings and one completely vegetarian. I had prepped the ingredients the night before, thinking that it would be a fairly easy process. My friend Monica and I started on our lentil stew journey early the next morning. We threw our ingredients together, brought them to a boil, and left the stews to simmer while bread warmed in the oven and we went to set the table.

Out of nowhere, we heard a loud *POP!* We ran into the kitchen and were shocked to find that the glass lid from my favorite pot had completely exploded! To this day, Monica and I recall how sad we felt as we both looked at that beautiful pot of lentil stew covered in tiny little glass pieces. Luckily, we had another one to eat, and to this day, I've never had a pot with a glass lid ever again!

Cooking is a process and a rewarding one at that. You start with something raw and sort of lifeless, and by adding heat, water, and air, you turn it into something completely magical and new. Among those key ingredients, though, is patience. You can't rush a dish into the oven, or make a stew in twenty minutes. Like life is (and like culinary school was), food is a practice in observation and repetition. You have to wait. You have to tend to the rich, wonderful, simple yet complicated stews of our lives—and be flexible enough to roll with the punches when little tiny glass pieces end up finding their way into the broth.

I think that's why a lot of people listen to music in the kitchen. You have to give the ingredients a chance to dance, too, while you wait in anticipation for the next steps and to relish the results.

FOOD IS STRENGTH.

I grew up listening to my mom tell everyone two things: that I cried a lot as a child (so much so that my cousins called me "la llorona," or the weeping woman) and that I had no upper body strength. I did a lot of sports as a child—gymnastics, swimming, handball, and ballet, and had almost started skating. But all the trainers I had always told my mom to make me exercise extra hard to build up my upper body strength.

I did, but it was never up to par.

It's funny how anything you hear as a child stays in your brain. To this day, I find myself telling people that I am not strong enough, that I lack upper body strength, and refer to my childhood stories to make a point.

After ten years of working for the Institute of Culinary Education and other places, I decided to create my own company back in the summer of 2014. I knew I wanted to teach cooking, especially to children, but I needed to pay the rent and make a living, so a more realistic plan needed to be in place.

My dream was Gaby's Kitchen: a mobile kitchen I could use to bring free food education to public schools in Jersey City. I did work volunteering for similar programs in New York City, so I thought I was going to be able to do it here, too. I was teaching a few classes and had gotten another one going for middle schoolers at a public school near me. But I needed to make money to pay my bills, so I began making empanadas at home to sell to friends. More and more people started asking for them. And then I took a leap of faith: I created a business, paid the city fees to have a vendor's license, passed the inspection, and cooked from a professional kitchen near my house. I sold the empanadas mostly to private customers and the occasional street fair or event I paid to attend.

Have you ever been so exhausted and tired that

you feel you are going to fall asleep standing up? I can only relate that tiredness to the times in college when I stayed up all night studying for a final, or when I had to work night shifts at a credit card data entry center. You basically live day in, day out in a prolonged battle against sleep deprivation. That's how I felt for the first two months I had my empanada "empire."

I sold a few different kinds: chicken with peppers and onions, spinach with onions in a bechamel sauce with cheese, ham and cheese, and, of course, the ones that most people remember and loved, my beef empanadas. My beef empanadas are the traditional porteñas from Buenos Aires. The beef is ground and mixed with the perfect balance of onions, peppers, and cumin. Cumin is the secret to an empanada's juiciness—at least according to my mother. That, and the copious amounts of oils and fat content of the meat. I also liked to put raisins and green olives in them, and traditionally, they have chopped hard-boiled eggs inside as well. (Although, that is something I started to pull away from since I realized a lot of people don't like eggs.

Besides, I always thought the egg felt like cheating on the beef. Probably the reason why it was added in the first place.)

Soon, my empanadas became the one thing the whole neighborhood talked about. I was exhausted but so happy. At one point, I even had a crazy idea of opening an empanada shack somewhere in Jersey City. After all, it wasn't going to be my first restaurant opening. A few years back, I helped my cousin open and manage a restaurant from the ground up in Puerto Escondido, Oaxaca, Mexico. It felt within reach. But at the time, it was financially impossible for me to do it, so I kept selling empanadas while continuing to teach.

Of course, my mom was there every step of the way. From the moment I had a website, she kept sending me messages to make sure the website worked. She also acted as my line cook and dishwasher. I never thought I would gather the physical strength I needed to get my business off the ground—let alone up and running. I did not have a car, so oftentimes we took taxis or had friends give us rides to various venues where I sold my food. We did almost everything by hand. We carried tables, chairs, banners, and the precious cargo themselves: the empanadas.

Those years as a vendor made me realize how much the amazing women I grew up with had embedded in me. They all had limitless creativity, curiosity, and above all, adaptability. They fixed things and figured out any obstacle, all the while acting as your marketing strategist, your sous-chef, and your closest confidante. These powerful women trained me to be strong—upper body strength be damned. I know now that I inherited some of that.

FOOD IS COURAGE.

Many times I've asked myself if an outcome of a certain situation had anything to do with my legal status, or the color of my skin, or my accent. Have I ever been treated differently for being Latina or treated with less respect?

Yes. Yes, and more than once. On top of it all, I am also treated differently for being a woman in a male-dominated industry where inflated egos weren't just a bad habit—they felt like a birthright. And if you are a woman in this industry and you have the balls to work in the back of the house, you are expected to work at the same pace as your male counterparts. That requires a lot of physical strength and mental work, learning to let things slide and not take anything personally.

Did I have awful moments? Yes. Did I cry? Oh, hell yes. I cried my eyes out so many days after working entire shifts in a kitchen. I worked hot, hungry, angry, sleep-deprived, hungover, you name it. After a few years and when I started having more confidence and courage to speak without feeling ridiculous about my accent, or my inability to lift a fifty-pound sack of potatoes, it did not bother me anymore. I learned to put my best foot forward and focus on the food and the relationships I was creating. I was able to find my place, partly because of "family meal."

Family meal, if you've never worked in a kitchen or a restaurant, is a free, preservice meal that the restaurant serves to the staff and is part of the perks of employment. You basically sit with all your coworkers, and for one hour, you act like a "family." You get to know more about the people you work with. Some restaurants use a part of the dining room; others don't have that luxury. Sometimes you end up sitting on a milk crate, and that is when you know you're in. When you do that, you know you belong to this work family.

Working in the kitchen, sometimes you have to make family meals for others, and it's an absolute roller coaster of emotions. If you are a prep cook, cooking for your peers can be nerve-racking the first couple of times. When you are on the line, there is a plan, a menu, a recipe. They show it to you a couple of times, and you repeat it day in, day out for a while until you can practically do it with your eyes closed. (Not recommended, but you know what I mean.) But when they ask you to tackle family meal, that is when you need a healthy dose of courage. Trust me on that one.

My first time making family meal at a restaurant was at Jack's Luxury Oyster Bar in the East Village. Chef Allison Vines-Rushing told me the day before, and then she proceeded to show me how she made dry pasta cooked like risotto. I was fresh out of culinary school, so I was very familiar on how to cook pasta, probably because I cooked and ate so many kinds of pasta at the time. But risotto was a whole other beast. Risotto is primarily an Italian dish and consists of stirring hot liquid (usually some sort of broth) into a mixture of rice with onions that has been previously sautéed in butter, adding the liquid in intervals while you stir continuously. Imagine my surprise when she asked me to do that with rigatoni, a tubular-shaped pasta!

I have to admit, I was skeptical at first. It wasn't about her. She was amazing, but I just didn't know if *I* could do it. It felt too new to me—outside the guidelines of what I'd ever been taught. I had to keep going and trust myself. It's in that split second, that moment when you make the decision to keep going, that courage becomes your guide. It happens again and again as you make more choices. I had to keep going and trust myself. I had to give in to the powers of the rigatoni risotto.

Which brings me to the *Bon Appétit* Test Kitchen. I remember my first week as test kitchen assistant at *Bon Appétit*. I started on June 13, 2016. It was a glorified dishwasher position. My back hurt so much from carrying heavy pots and pans, and trays of dirty utensils all day long. They provided tools to make it easier, like a pushcart and some bins, but the job was insane. I was wet all day with a mix of dishwater and sweat. But I was in the test kitchen of a food magazine

I'd admired for so long. I was surrounded by amazing recipes all day, got to talk about food, breathe food, and best of all, I was able to taste it!

So I kept showing up for those hard days that turned into the dream job—test kitchen manager—and I loved it! I am so thankful for what *was* good about that place and what made it "the dream."

While it takes courage to plunge yourself into the unknown, it takes even more to know when it's time to move on and leave what seems to be a dream job. Perhaps it is easier said than done, but a lot happened in the summer of 2020. I wanted to prove once again what I'm made of. I got tired of waiting for the world to turn around and show up for me—and also tired of people that took me for granted. I am a chef. I am a professionally trained chef. I have years of experience cooking, teaching, and enduring. I got sidetracked a few times, yes. But at the end of the day, the feeling is still the same. I wanted, and continue to want, to share my knowledge with people that love food just as much as I do. And I thought it was time to get back to that.

I wish someone had told me that changing your mind was fine. That choosing a different path was okay, that your final goals can change on the go, and the path to achievement is not created equal for everyone, but is just as valuable in its uniqueness. That it's all just circumstances; not only yours, but of the lives of the ones before you, that end up bringing you to where you are now. If you just keep going.

FOOD IS LOVE.

Oftentimes, I ask "Comistes?" ("Have you eaten yet?") before I say "Hello." You have to understand that it is not just a result of an ever-curious mind, although that surely plays a part. It is out of a deep, deep love for every aspect of cooking, down to the very atoms. Cooking, eating at a table, sharing that time of relaxation and nourishment are acts of serious, unconditional love. Nothing unites us more than sitting at a table with others. It is one of those funny things that's taken for granted, that we sometimes don't appreciate enough.

Life, like cooking food, is made of little parts, different items or ingredients that you put together because you think they will get along great. Then something happens, and you shift your gears and go in a different direction. Finally, the dish is so good, so memorable, that you need to write it down, like a story, because you want to cook it again. You want to be able to relive that moment and savor it forever.

Have you ever felt like you have so much to share, so much to give, so much to say that your head and your heart were going to burst? That's how I feel about food. I want to cook and I want to teach. I want to talk and I always want to share. I've learned so many things in life, not only in school but from people, from friends, from my mom and my abuelas, my coworkers, and my teachers. I am still learning, and I still *want* to learn more. Because this exchange of knowledge is, in fact, love. Nothing makes me happier than when someone says "I cooked this! I learned it from you" after I teach a class or share a video.

I went from being a nanny and cleaning homes to working as a waitress, a line cook, and a dishwasher to creating my own little company and carving out a space in the culinary world that felt right *for me*. It wasn't easy. There were ups and downs. There were times I almost gave up and settled.

But at the end of it all, there was adventure, patience, courage, strength, and love. Those are the fundamental ingredients to doing it right. The rest is just gravy. (But I still want you to have the full meal, and dessert, too.)

Buen provecho! Keep cooking. Be happy.

ABOUT US

Pocket Change Collective was born out of a need for space. Space to think. Space to connect. Space to be yourself. And this is your invitation to join us.

These books are small, but they are mighty. They ask big questions and propose even bigger solutions. They show us that no matter where we come from or where we're going, we can all take part in changing the communities around us. Because the possibilities of how we can use our space for good are endless.

So thank you. Thank you for picking this book up. Thank you for reading. Thank you for being a part of the Pocket Change Collective.

 63